Corel Quattro Pro
Keyboard Shortcuts

By

U. C-Abel Books.

Published by U. C-Abel Books

Table of Contents

Acknowledgement.

We return all glory to God Almighty for enabling us to bring this work to this point.

We sincerely appreciate the great company called Corel Corporation for their hard work and way of reasoning in terms of providing their customers with helpful programs and resources, and for helping us with some of the tips and keyboard shortcuts included in this book. We also remember our lovely readers who are never tired of reading our publications.

We really wish you well.

Dedication

We pleasurably dedicate this title to Corel Quattro Pro users all over the world.

Introduction

After thinking of how to help computer users become more productive in their operation of computers and various fields, it came to our knowledge that there is a smart option many computer users ignore easily and that part has a high yielding capacity that is known to just few people.

We went into a deep research to broaden our knowledge of key combination and found it very helpful, then we started this series "Shortcut Matters" including tips, techniques, keyboard shortcuts, and packaging the title in a way it will attract readers and get a high rating class.

As people who love keyboard shortcuts we treat each topic plainly in an easy-to-read way even to the understanding of a lay man.

Relax and make your mind ready for learning as we go.

What to Know Before You Begin.

General Notes.

1. Most of the keyboard shortcuts you will see in this book refer to the U.S. keyboard layout. Keys for other layouts might not correspond exactly to the keys on a U.S. keyboard. Keyboard shortcuts for laptop computers might also differ.

2. It is important to note that when using shortcuts to perform any command, you should make sure the target area is active, if not, you may get a wrong result. Example, if you want to highlight all texts you must make sure the text field is active and if an object, make sure the object area is active. The active area is always known by the location where the cursor of your computer blinks.

3. On a Mac keyboard, the Command key is denoted with the ⌘symbol.

4. If a function key doesn't work on your Mac as you expect it to, press the Fn key in addition to the function key. If you don't want to press the Fn key every time, you can change your Apple system preferences.

5. The plus (+) sign that comes in the middle of keyboard shortcuts simply means the keys are meant to be combined or held down together not to be added as one of the shortcut keys. In a case where plus sign is needed; it will be duplicated (++).

6. Many keyboards assign special functions to function keys, by default. To use the function key for other purposes, you have to press Fn+the function key.

7. For keyboard shortcuts in which you press one key immediately followed by another key, the keys are separated by a comma (,).

8. For chapters that have more than one topic, search for "A fresh topic" to see the beginning of a topic, and "End of Topic" to see the end of a topic.

9. It is also important to note that the keyboard shortcuts listed in this book are to be used in Corel Quattro Pro.

10. To get more information on this title visit ucabelbooks.wordpress.com and search the site using keywords related to it.

11. Our chief website is under construction.

Some Short Forms You Will Find in This Book and Their Full Meaning.

Here are short forms used in this Corel Quattro Pro Keyboard Shortcuts book and their full meaning.

1.	Win	-	Windows logo key
2.	Tab	-	Tabulate Key
3.	Shft	-	Shift Key
4.	Prt sc	-	Print Screen
5.	Num Lock	-	Number Lock Key
6.	F	-	Function Key
7.	Esc	-	Escape Key
8.	Ctrl	-	Control Key
9.	Caps Lock	-	Caps Lock Key
10.	Alt	-	Alternate Key

CHAPTER 1.

Fundamental Knowledge of Keyboard Shortcuts.

Without the existence of the keyboard, there wouldn't have been anything like keyboard shortcuts so in this chapter we will learn a little about the computer keyboard before moving to keyboard shortcuts.

1. Definition of Computer Keyboard.

This is an input device that is used to send data to computer memory.

Sketch of a Keyboard

1.1 Types of Keyboard.

i. Standard (Basic) Keyboard.

ii. Enhanced (Extended) Keyboard.

i. **Standard Keyboard:** This is a keyboard designed during the 1800s for mechanical typewriters with just 10 function keys (F keys) placed at the left side of it.

ii. **Enhanced Keyboard:** This is the current 101 to 102-key keyboard that is included in almost all the personal computers (PCs) of nowadays, which has 12 function keys, usually at the top side of it.

Function Keys

Numeric Keys

Alphabetic keys

1.2 Segments of the keyboard

- Numeric keys.
- Alphabetic keys.
- Punctuation keys.
- Windows Logo key.
- Function keys.
- Special keys.

Numeric Keys: Numeric keys are keys with numbers from **0 - 9**.

Alphabetic Keys: These are keys that have alphabets on them, ranging from **A** to **Z**.

Punctuation Keys: These are keys of the keyboard used for punctuation, examples include comma, full stop, colon, question marks, hyphen, etc.

Windows Logo Key: A key on Microsoft Computer keyboard with its logo displayed on it. Search for this 🪟 on your keyboard.

Apple Key: This also known as Command key is a modifier key that you can find on an Apple keyboard. It usually has the image of an apple or command logo on it. Search for this on your Apple keyboard ⌘

Function Keys: These are keys that have **F** on them which are usually combined with other keys. They are F1 - F12, and are also in the class called *Special Keys*.

Special Keys: These are keys that perform special functions. They include: Tab, Ctrl, Caps lock, Insert, Prt sc, alt gr, Shift, Home, Num lock, Esc, and many others. Special keys differ according to the type of computer involved. In some keyboard layout, especially laptops, the keys that turn the speaker on/off, the one that increases/decreases volume, the key that turns the computer Wifi on/off are also special keys.

Other Special Keys Worthy of Note.

Enter Key: This is located at the right-hand corner of most keyboards. It is used to send messages to the computer to execute commands, in most cases it is used to mean "Ok" or "Go".

Escape Key (ESC): This is the first key on the upper left of most keyboards. It is used to cancel routines, close menus and select options such as **Save** according to circumstances.

Control Key (CTRL): It is located on the bottom row of the left and right hand side of the keyboard. They also work with the function keys to execute commands using Keyboard shortcuts (key combinations).

Alternate Key (ALT): It is located on the bottom row also of some keyboard, very close to the CTRL key on both side of the keyboard. It enables many editing functions to be accomplished by using some keystroke combinations on the keyboard.

Shift Key: This adds to the roles of function keys. In addition, it enables the use of alternative function of a particular button (key), especially, those with more than one function on a key. E.g. use of capital letters, symbols, and numbers.

1.3. Selecting/Highlighting With Keyboard.

This is a highlighting method or style where data is selected using the computer keyboard instead of a computer mouse.

To do this:

- Move your cursor to the text or object you want to highlight, make sure that area is active,
- Hold down the shift key with one finger,
- Then use another finger to move the arrow key that points to the direction you want to highlight.

1.4 The Operating Modes Of The Keyboard.

Just like the computer mouse, keyboard has two operating modes. The two modes are Text Entering Mode and Command Mode.

a. **Text Entering Mode:** this mode gives the operator/user the opportunity to type text.
b. **Command Mode:** this is used to command the operating system/software/application to execute commands in certain ways.

2. Ways To Improve In Your Typing Skill.

1. Put Your Eyes Off The Keyboard.

This is the aspect of keyboard usage that many don't find funny because they always ask. "How can I put my eyes off the keyboard when I am running away from the occurrence of errors on my file?" My aim is to be fast, is this not going to slow me down?

Of course, there will be errors and at the same time your speed will slow down but the motive behind the introduction to this method is to make you faster than you are. Looking at your keyboard while you type can make you get a sore neck, it is better you learn to touch type because the more you type with your eyes fixed on the screen instead of the keyboard, the faster you become.

An alternative to keeping your eyes off your keyboard is to use the "*Das Keyboard Ultimate*".

2. Errors Challenge You

It is better to fail than to not try at all. Not trying at all is an attribute of the weak and lazybones. When you make mistakes, try again because errors are opportunities for improvement.

3. Good Posture (Position Yourself Well).

Do not adopt an awkward position while typing. You should get everything on your desk organized or arranged before sitting to type. Your posture while typing contributes to your speed and productivity.

4. Practice

Here is the conclusion of everything said above. You have to practice your shortcuts constantly. The practice alone is a way of improvement. "Practice brings improvement". Practice always.

2.1 Software That Will Help You Improve Your Typing Skill.

There are several Software programs for typing that both kids and adults can use for their typing skill. Here is a list of software that can help you improve in your typing: Mavis Beacon, Typing Instructor, Mucky Typing Adventure, Rapid Tying Tutor, Letter Chase Tying Tutor, Alice Touch Typing Tutor and many more. Personally, I love Mavis Beacon.

To learn typing using MAVIS BEACON, install Mavis Beacon software to your computer, start with keyboard lesson, then move to games. Games like *Penguin Crossing, Creature Lab*, or *Space Junk* will help you become a professional in typing. Typing and keyboard shortcuts work hand-in-hand.

Sketch of a computer mouse

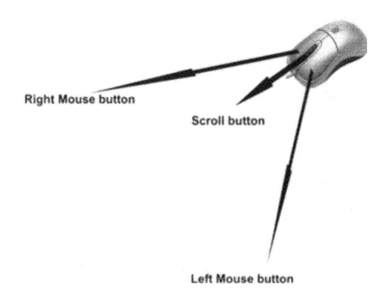

Right Mouse button

Scroll button

Left Mouse button

3. Mouse:

This is an oval-shaped portable input device with three buttons for scrolling, left clicking, and right clicking that enables work to be done effectively on a computer. The plural form of mouse is mice.

3.1 Types of Computer Mouse

- Mechanical Mouse.
- Optical Mechanical Mouse (Optomechanical).
- Laser Mouse.
- Optical Mouse.

- BlueTrack Mouse.

3.2 Forms of Clicking:

Left Clicking: This is the process of clicking the left side button of the mouse. It can also be called *clicking* without the addition of *left*.

Right Clicking: It is the process of clicking the right side button of a computer mouse.

Double Clicking: It is the process of clicking the left side button two times (twice) and immediately.

Triple Clicking: It is the process of clicking the left side button three times (thrice) and immediately.

Double clicking is used to select a word while triple clicking is used to select a sentence or paragraph.

Scroll Button: It is the little key attached to the mouse that looks like a tiny wheel. It takes you up and down a page when moved.

3.3 Mouse Pad: This is a small soft mat that is placed under the mouse to make it have a free movement.

3.4 Laptop Mouse Touchpad

This unlike the mouse we explained above is not external, rather it is inbuilt (comes with the laptop computer). With the presence of a laptop mouse touchpad, an external mouse is not needed to use a laptop, except in a case where it is malfunctioning or the operator prefers to use external one for some reasons.

The laptop mouse touchpad is usually positioned at the end of the keyboard section of a laptop computer. It is rectangular in shape with two buttons positioned below it. The two buttons/keys are used for left and right clicking just like the external mouse. Some laptops come with four mouse keys. Two placed above the mouse for left and right clicking and two other keys placed below it for the same function.

4. Definition Of Keyboard Shortcuts.

Keyboard shortcuts are defined as a series of keys, most times with combination that execute tasks which typically involve the use of mouse or other input devices.

5. Why You Should Use Shortcuts.

1. One may not be able to use a computer mouse easily because of disability or pain.

2. One may not be able to see the mouse pointer as a result of vision impairment, in such case what will the person do? The answer is SHORTCUT.

3. Research has made it known that Extensive mouse usage is related to Repetitive Syndrome Injury (RSI) greatly than the use of keyboard.

4. Keyboard shortcuts speed up computer users, making learning them a worthwhile effort.

5. When performing a job that requires precision, it is wise that you use the keyboard instead of mouse, for instance, if you are dealing with Text Editing, it is better you handle it using keyboard shortcuts than spending more time doing it with your computer mouse alone.

6. Studies calculate that using keyboard shortcuts allows working 10 times faster than working with the mouse. The time you spend looking for the mouse and then getting the cursor to the position you want is lost! Reducing your work duration by 10 times gives you greater results.

5.1 Ways To Become A Lover Of Shortcuts.

1. Always have the urge to learn new shortcut keys associated with the programs you use.
2. Be happy whenever you learn a new shortcut.
3. Try as much as you can to apply the new shortcuts you learnt.

4. Always bear it in mind that learning new shortcuts is worth it.
5. Always remember that the use of keyboard shortcuts keeps people healthy while performing computer activities.

5.2 How To Learn New Shortcut Keys
1. Do a research on them: quick references (a cheat sheet comprehensively compiled like ours) can go a long way to help you improve.
2. Buy applications that show you keyboard shortcuts every time you execute an action with mouse.
3. Disconnect your mouse if you must learn this fast.
4. Read user manuals and help topics (Whether offline or online).

5.3 Your Reward For Knowing Shortcut Keys.
1. You will get faster unimaginably.
2. Your level of efficiency will increase.
3. You will find it easy to use.
4. Opportunities are high that you will become an expert in what you do.
5. You won't have to go for **Office button**, click **New,** click **Blank and Recent**, and click **Create** just to insert a fresh/blank page. **Ctrl +N** takes care of that in a second.

A Funny Note: Keyboarding and Mousing are in a marital union with Keyboarding being the head, so it will be unfair for anybody to put asunder between them.

5.4 Why We Emphasize On The Use of Shortcuts.

You may never leave your mouse completely unless you are ready to make your brain a box of keyboard shortcuts which will really be frustrating, just imagine yourself learning all shortcuts that go with the programs you use and their various versions. You shouldn't learn keyboard shortcuts that way.

Why we are emphasizing on the use of shortcuts is because mouse usage is becoming unusually common and unhealthy, too. So we just want to make sure both are combined so you can get fast, productive and healthy in your computer activities. All you need to know is just the most important ones associated with the programs you use.

CHAPTER 2.

15 (Fifteen) Special Keyboard Shortcuts.

The fifteen special keyboard shortcuts are fifteen (15) shortcuts every computer user should know.

The following is a list of keyboard shortcuts every computer user should know:

1. **Ctrl + A:** Control A, highlights or selects everything you have in the environment where you are working.

    *If you are like **"Wow, the content of this document is large and there is no time to select all of it, besides, it's going to mount pressure on my computer?"** Using the mouse for this is an outdated method of handling a task like selecting all, Ctrl+A will take care of that in a second.*

2. **Ctrl + C:** Control C copies any highlighted or selected element within the work environment.

    Saves the time and stress which would have been used to right click and click again just to copy. Use ctrl+c.

3. **Ctrl + N:** Control N opens a new window or file.

    *Instead of clicking **File**, **New**, **blank/ template** and another **click**, just press **Ctrl + N** and a fresh page or window will appear instantly.*

4. **Ctrl + O:** Control O opens a new program.

    Use ctrl +O when you want to locate / open a file or program.

5. **Ctrl + P:** Control P prints the active document.

    Always use this to locate the printer dialog box, and thereafter print.

6. **Ctrl + S:** Control S saves a new document or file and changes made by the user.

    Please stop! Don't use the mouse. Just press Ctrl+S and everything will be saved.

7. **Ctrl +V:** Control V pastes copied elements into the active area of the program in use.

Using ctrl+V in a case like this Saves the time and stress of right clicking and clicking again just to paste.

8. **Ctrl + W:** Control W is used to close the page you are working on when you want to leave the work environment.

    "There is a way Debby does this without using the mouse. Oh my God, why didn't I learn it then?" Don't worry, I have the answer. Debby presses Ctrl+W to close active windows.

9. **Ctrl + X:** Control X cuts elements (making the elements to disappear from their original place). The difference between cutting and deleting elements is that in Cutting, what was cut doesn't get lost permanently but prepares itself so that it can be pasted on another location defined by the user.

    *Use ctrl+x when you think **"this shouldn't be here and I can't stand the stress of retyping or redesigning it on the rightful place it belongs".***

10. **Ctrl + Y:** Control Y undoes already done actions.

Ctrl+Z brought back what you didn't need? Press Ctrl+ Y to remove it again.

11. **Ctrl + Z:** Control Z redoes actions.
Can't find what you typed now or a picture you inserted, it suddenly disappeared or you mistakenly removed it? Press Ctrl+Z to bring it back.

12. **Alt + F4:** Alternative F4 closes active windows or items.

    *You don't need to move the mouse in order to close an active window, just press **Alt + F4**. Also use it when you are done or you don't want somebody who is coming to see what you are doing.*

13. **Ctrl + F6:** Control F6 Navigates between open windows, making it possible for a user to see what is happening in windows that are active.
Are you working in Microsoft Word and want to find out if the other active window where your browser is loading a page is still progressing? Use Ctrl + F6.

14. **F1:** This displays the help window.

*Is your computer malfunctioning? Use **F1** to find help when you don't know what next to do.*

15. **F12:** This enables user to make changes to an already saved document.
    F12 is the shortcut to use when you want to change the format in which you saved your existing document, password it, change its name, change the file location or destination, or make other changes to it. It will save you time.

Note: The Control (Ctrl) key on Windows and Linux operating system is the same thing as Command (Cmmd) key on a Macintosh computer. So if you replace Control with Command key on a Mac computer for the special shortcuts listed above, you will get the same result.

CHAPTER 3.

Tips, Tricks, Techniques, and Keyboard Shortcuts for use in WordPerfect Quattro Pro.

About the program: This is a spreadsheet program developed by Borland and now sold by Corel Corporation.

A fresh topic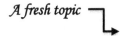

Drawing Arrows in Quattro Pro.

Drawing shapes and lines enhances the look of a spreadsheet. For example, you can use arrows to highlight the relations between cells and objects.

	A	B	C	D	E
1	Continent	Area (in sq km)			
2	Asia	44579000			
3	Africa	30065000			
4	North America	24256000			
5	South America	17819000			
6	Antarctica	13209000			
7	Europe	9938000			
8	Australia/Oceania	7687000	⬅ Smallest continent		
9					
10					
11					
12					
13					
14					
15					

You can access tools for drawing arrows from the Drawing tools toolbar. Other shapes available in Quattro Pro® include squares, flowchart shapes, callout shapes, and stars.

To display the Drawing tools toolbar

1. Click **View > Toolbars**.

2. Enable the **Drawing tools** check box in the **Toolbar** list.

The Drawing tools toolbar.

To draw an arrow shape

1. Open the arrow shapes flyout on the Drawing tools toolbar.

2. Choose an arrow shape.

3. Drag in the spreadsheet to create the arrow.

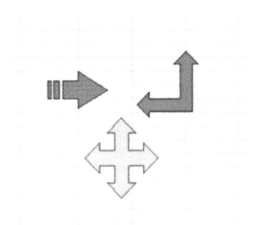

4. Change any properties on the property bar.

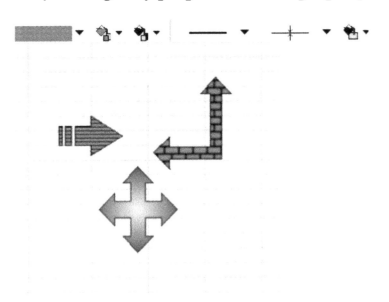

Using variables to save time and reduce errors

To save you time when creating a document, WordPerfect® lets you insert variables. Variables allow you to mark text that you know will change — for example, dates, version numbers, or client names. Using variables for certain text strings can also save you from the tedium of repetition and eliminate the errors that result when something needs to be typed multiple times.

To appreciate the benefits of using variables, consider the task of writing an article about the WordPerfect Office suite. In your article, the name of each application may appear with or without a version number. In addition, each application may be appear with or without trademarking symbols (for example, "WordPerfect® 12" or "WordPerfect 12").

Variables can help you achieve significant time savings, especially when product names and version numbers aren't set in stone. It's easy to make changes to a variable and have the changes immediately reflected throughout a document.

To create a variable

Before you start a document, it's a good idea to identify the circumstances in which you might find variables useful. For this tip, we'll create variables that differentiate the application names and trademarks of the WordPerfect Office suite.

1. In WordPerfect, click **Insert > Variable**.

2. In the **Variables** dialog box, click **Create**.

3. In the **Variables Editor** dialog box (see below), type a name for the variable in the **Variable** box. For WordPerfect Office 12, for example, I've typed "WPO12".

4. Type a description in the **Description** box. The description you choose might simply be an identifier that helps you distinguish between variables. For this example, I've typed "suite name".

5. In the **Contents** area, type the text that you want to display whenever you insert this variable in a document. For this example, I've typed "WordPerfect Office 12".

6. Click **OK**.

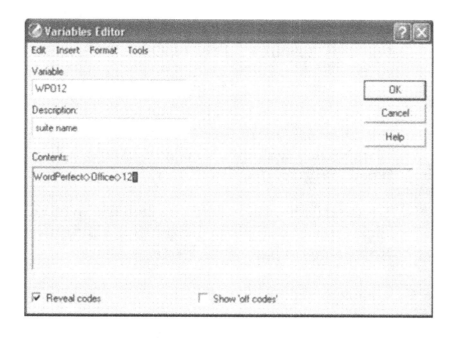

The **Variables Editor** dialog box lets you create, edit, and apply text formatting attributes to variables.

Next, we need to create a trademarked variable of the suite name.

1. In the **Variables** dialog box, click **Create**.

2. In the **Variables Editor** dialog box, type a name for the **variable** in the Variable box. Because this variable contains a trademarking symbol, I've used "TM: WPO12".

3. Type a description in the **Description** box. For this example, I've typed "trademarked suite".

4. In the **Contents** area, type the text that you want to display whenever you insert this variable in a document. For this example, I've typed "WordPerfect® Office 12".

5. To insert the registered trademark symbol, click **Insert > Symbol** from the **Variables Editor** menu bar, or click **Ctrl + W**.

6. Click **OK**.

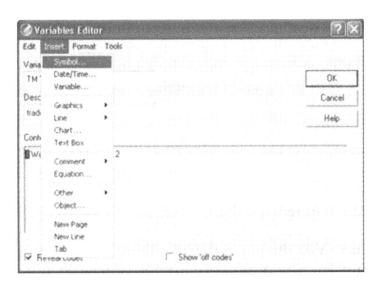

The **Variables Editor** dialog box lets you apply to variables the same formatting attributes that are available in a regular WordPerfect document, including the insertion of symbols.

At this point, we could continue to create variables for Presentations™ and Quattro Pro®. For the sake of efficiency, however, we'll proceed to inserting variables into documents.

To insert a variable

1. Position the cursor where you want to insert the variable.
2. Click **Insert > Variable**.
3. In the **Variables** dialog box, choose a variable from the **Variable** list.
4. Click **Insert**.

The **Variables** dialog box lets you choose which variable you want to insert in a document.

End of Topic.

A fresh topic

Using QuickPaste in Quattro Pro®.

As you work with data in Quattro Pro®, you might have to move cells around the spreadsheet. The QuickPaste feature lets you automatically insert the correct number of cells for the data you copy or cut from one area to another. QuickPaste gives you exceptional control when pasting data. You can choose to simply paste the copied cells, which will displace existing cells. Or, you can insert new rows or columns so that existing cells remain in their original rows or columns.

Displacing existing cells.

You can easily paste cells into a spreadsheet so that existing cells are displaced by the number of cells you're pasting. You have the option of displacing existing cells to the right or down. This forces existing data into rows or columns that didn't contain data.

1. Select the cells containing the data you want to copy.

2. Click **Edit > Copy**.

3. Select the upper leftmost cell where you want to paste the copied data and cells.

4. Right-click, and click **QuickPaste**.

5. In the **QuickPaste** dialog box, enable the **Partial** option in the **Span** area. The range of affected cells is displayed in the **Cells** box. You can highlight the affected cells that will be affected by clicking the **Range picker** button ▪ beside the **Cells** box.

6. In the **Dimension** area, enable one of the following options:
   • **Columns** — shifts cells to the right
   • **Rows** — shifts cells down

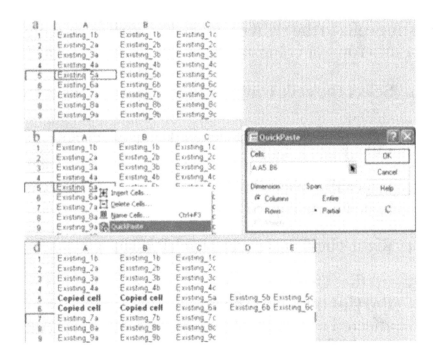

Figure 1

This is an example of: a) existing cells in a spreadsheet; b) accessing QuickPaste through the shortcut menu; c) setting options in the QuickPaste dialog box; d) pasting displaces existing cells.

Keeping existing cells in their original rows or columns

You can insert new rows or columns as you use QuickPaste, which keeps existing cells in their existing rows or columns. The only data in the new rows or columns is the cells you pasted.

1. Select the cells containing the data you want to copy.

2. Click **Edit > Copy**.

3. Select the upper leftmost cell where you want to paste the copied data and cells.

4. Right-click, and click **QuickPaste**.

5. In the **QuickPaste** dialog box, enable the **Entire** option in the **Span** area.

6. In the **Dimension** area, enable one of the following options:
   • **Columns** — inserts as many columns in the spreadsheet as there are in the copied data and shifts cells to the right
   • **Rows** — inserts as many rows in the spreadsheet as there are in the copied data and shifts cells down

	A	B	C
1	Existing_1b	Existing_1b	Existing_1c
2	Existing_2a	Existing_2b	Existing_2c
3	Existing_3a	Existing_3b	Existing_3c
4	Existing_4a	Existing_4b	Existing_4c
5	Copied cell	Copied cell	
6	Copied cell	Copied cell	
7	Existing_5a	Existing_5b	Existing_5c
8	Existing_6a	Existing_6b	Existing_6c

Figure
This is an example of copying cells in new rows and inserting existing data.

End of Topic.

A fresh topic ⌐
          ↳

Keyboard Shortcuts for use in WordPerfect Quattro Pro.

Quattro Pro can display keyboard shortcuts beside each menu command in the menu bar. You can disable this feature if you do not want shortcuts displayed.

You can customize many of the keyboard shortcuts. For more information about customizing keyboard shortcuts, see "Customizing keyboards."

Depending on what mode you are in keyboard shortcuts may be repeated but their functions change.

Shortcuts for Common Tasks.

The following list is made up of keyboard shortcuts you can use to boost your productivity in Corel Quattro Pro.

SHORTCUT	TASK
Alt + (underscored letter)	Opens relevant menu. For example, pressing **Alt + F** opens the **File** menu.
underscored letter	Once a menu is open, press the underscored letter alone to select a command. For example, if the **File** menu is open, pressing **P** selects the **Print** command.
Alt, then Ctrl + Tab	Selects the first item on the first toolbar. Press **Tab** to move the focus to the right, press **Shift + Tab** to move it to the left, and press **Spacebar** to select an command. Press **Ctrl + Tab** again to move to the next toolbar.
Ctrl + N	File ▶ New
Ctrl + O	File ▶ Open
Ctrl + F4	File ▶ Close
Ctrl + S	File ▶ Save
F3	File ▶ Save as
Alt + F + G	File ▶ Page setup
Ctrl + P	File ▶ Print
Alt + F4	File ▶ Exit

Ctrl + Z	Edit ▸ Undo
Ctrl + Shift + Z	Edit ▸ Redo
Ctrl + X, or Shift + Del	Edit ▸ Cut
Ctrl + C, or Ctrl + Ins	Edit ▸ Copy
Ctrl + V, or Shift + Ins	Edit ▸ Paste
Ctrl + B	Makes selected text bold
Ctrl + I	Makes selected text italic
Ctrl + E	Centers selected text
Ctrl + U	Underlines selected text
Ctrl + L	Left aligns selected text
Ctrl + R	Right aligns selected text
Backspace	Erases the character to the left of the cursor when the cursor is in a cell. Erases everything in a cell when the cell is selected.
Spacebar	Enables or disables the area within the cursor's focus (such as check boxes or links in a list)
Caps lock	Enters Caps mode, in which all letters you type are displayed in uppercase letters. Press again to exit Caps mode
Ctrl + D	Inserts the date
Ctrl + Enter	Inserts a hard page break
Ctrl + Break	If pressed while a macro is executing, terminates the macro

Del	Erases the contents (but not properties) of the current cell or selected cells
Ctrl + Del	In Group mode, acts like **Del**, but "drills" the deletion through the group (deletes the selected cell, cells, or graphics on all grouped spreadsheets)
\ (Backslash)	Lets you type one or more characters to repeat across an entire cell width
Enter	In a notebook, writes the entry on the input line into the current cell, and returns to Ready mode. In a menu, choice list, or dialog box, chooses the selected item.
Esc	Cancels whatever task you are doing. For example, it can back you out of a menu, exit a dialog box, or erase any changes you made in the input line.
Num lock	Toggles performance of the numeric keypad keys between numeric keys and **Arrow** keys
Pause	Enters Macro Debug mode
Scroll lock	Toggles performance of the **Arrow** keys. When you first press **Scroll lock**, the **SCRL** indicator is enabled on the status bar and the **Arrow** keys scroll the

	contents of the active window without changing which cell is selected. When you press **Scroll lock** again, you can change which cell is selected with the **Arrow** keys.
Ctrl + Page down or Page up	In a notebook, moves from one spreadsheet to the next or previous spreadsheet. In a dialog box with multiple settings, changes panes (groups of property options).
Ctrl + Shift + Page down or Page up	Lets you selects multiple spreadsheets
Up or Down Arrow	In a dialog box text box, enters Point mode.
Tab	In a notebook, moves right one column. In a dialog box, moves between controls. In a Help window, use to move between jumps, and press **Enter** to select jumps.
Ctrl + Tab	In a graphics window, press **Ctrl + Tab** to select an object in the chart.
Shift + Tab	In a notebook, moves left one cell. In a dialog box, moves to the previous control. In a graphics window, moves to the beginning

	of the current word in a text box. Use **Ctrl + Shift + Tab** to select the previous item in a chart.
Ctrl + Left Arrow	In a notebook, moves left one screen
Ctrl + Right Arrow	In a notebook, moves right one screen
Ctrl + Shift + F	Displays the **SpeedFormat** dialog box
Ctrl + W	Displays the **Symbols** dialog box
Ctrl + Shift + L	Displays a list of series names from which you can choose to fill cells. Equivalent to clicking the **QuickFill** button on the notebook bar.
Ctrl + Shift + S	Activates the **Styles** list box on the property bar
Ctrl + Shift + N	Equivalent to clicking **File ▸ New from template**. Displays the PerfectExpert.
Alt + Down Arrow	In box, in a dialog box, with a **Browse** button, activates the **Open File** dialog box.
Ctrl + F	Opens the **Find and replace** dialog box

Edit Mode Keys.

The following keys are available in Edit mode.

SHORTCUT	TASK
Esc	Exits Edit mode. If you click **Tools ▸ Settings**, and in the list of categories, double-click **Workspace**, **Application** and click **General**, and then enable the **Compatible keys** check box, pressing **Esc** erases the contents of the input line, and pressing **Esc** a second time exits Edit mode.
Enter	Enters the data and exits Edit mode
Ctrl + Enter	In Group mode, acts like **Enter**, but "drills" data through all grouped spreadsheets at once
Up Arrow	If data is wrapped on more than one line, moves the cursor up a line. If you click **Tools ▸ Settings**, and in the list of categories, double-click **Workspace**, **Application** and click **General**, and then enable the **Compatible keys** check box, pressing **Up Arrow** enters the data, exits Edit mode, and moves up one cell. When the cursor follows an

	operator in a formula, enters Point mode.
Down Arrow	If data is wrapped on more than one line, moves the cursor down a line. If you click **Tools ▸ Settings**, and in the list of categories, double-click **Workspace**, **Application** and click **General**, and then enable the **Compatible keys** check box, **Down Arrow** enters the data, exits Edit mode, and moves down one cell. When the cursor follows an operator in a formula, enters Point mode.
Page down	Enters the data, exits Edit mode, and moves down one screen. When the cursor follows an operator in a formula, enters Point mode.
Page up	Enters the data, exits Edit mode, and moves up one screen. When the cursor follows an operator in a formula, enters Point mode.
Ins	Toggles between Insert and Overwrite modes (Insert is the default)
Backspace	Deletes characters to the left of the cursor

Del	Deletes characters to the right of the cursor, selected cells, or a graphic
Ctrl + Backspace	Erases the contents of the input line
Ctrl + Right Arrow	Moves to the next page
Tab	Moves to the next cell. The cursor moves to the next page if you click **Tools ▸ Settings**, and in the list of categories, double-click **Workspace**, **Application** and click **General**, and then enable the **Compatibility keys** check box.
Shift + Tab	Moves to the previous cell
Ctrl + Left Arrow	Moves to the next page
Ctrl + Shift + Right Arrow	Selects content from the cursor to the next page.
Ctrl + Shift + Left Arrow	Selects content from the cursor to the previous page.
F2	Toggles to display an indicator on the application bar that tells you what type of data you are editingeither value or label
Shift + F3	Displays a list of macro commands
Alt + F3	Displays a list of spreadsheet functions

F9	Calculates and then displays formula results on the input line

Object Keys.

The following list describes the shortcut keys available when working with objects, such as shapes, charts, and maps.

SHORTCUT	TASK
Spacebar + Arrow keys	Controls horizontal and vertical pointer movement when you draw an object. If an object is selected, lets you control the object's movement.
Spacebar + Home	Moves the pointer up and left diagonally when you draw an object. If an object is selected, moves the object up and left diagonally.
Spacebar + Page up	Moves the pointer up and right diagonally when you draw an object. If an object is selected, moves the object up and right diagonally.
Spacebar + End	Moves the pointer down and left diagonally when you draw an object. If an object is selected,

	moves the object down and left diagonally.
Spacebar + Page down	Moves the pointer down and right diagonally when you draw an object. If an object is selected, moves the object down and right diagonally.
Ctrl +]	Selects the object that was created first on the active spreadsheet, and selects the remaining objects in the order in which they were created
Ctrl + [	Selects the object that was created last on the active spreadsheet, and selects the remaining objects in the reverse order in which they were created
F12	Opens a dialog box specific to the object selected
Esc	Closes the current dialog box. Also cancels the selection of a selected object.
Delete	Deletes the selected object

Formula Composer Keys.

The following list describes the shortcut keys available when working in the formula outline pane of the Formula Composer.

SHORTCUT	TASK
Ctrl + Plus sign	Expands the outline by one level
Ctrl + Shift + 8	Expands the whole outline for the formula
Ctrl + Minus sign	Collapses the current branch of the outline
Ctrl + F	Goes to a referenced cell in the formula
Ctrl + B	Returns to the previous cell containing a formula that references the current cell
Ctrl + E	Converts the current expression to a value
Ctrl + O	Replaces the current expression with an @function
Ctrl + P	Switches to Point mode to specify a cell reference by pointing to a cell (or cells) on a spreadsheet
Ctrl + N	Replaces the current expression with a cell name

Point Mode Keys.

The following keys are available in Point mode.

SHORTCUT	TASK
Arrow keys + Period key	Press the **Arrow** keys to select the first cell and press the period key.

	Press the **Arrow** keys to move to the last cell you want to select.
Enter	Enters the selected cells in the formula or dialog box and, exits Point mode
Esc	If pressed while pointing to cells, returns you to the anchor cell
Backspace	If pressed while pointing to cells, returns you to the cell that was active before you entered Point mode
F4	Makes the cell address to the left of the cursor absolute. Press repeatedly to cycle through the absolute combinations; for example, $A:$B$4, $A:B$4. (Does not disturb the selected cell.)
Alt + F5	Turns Group mode on or off
F6	If the window is split into two panes, jumps to the other pane
Ctrl + F6	If multiple windows are open, jumps to the next window

Print Preview Keys.

The following table lists keys you can use while previewing.

SHORTCUT	TASK
Esc	Exits the preview
F1	Displays online Help
Page up	Displays the previous spreadsheet
Page down	Displays the next spreadsheet
+ (plus key)	Zooms in a level, increasing detail
- (minus key)	Zooms out a level, decreasing detail
Up Arrow	Scrolls a zoomed display up
Down Arrow	Scrolls a zoomed display down
Right Arrow	Scrolls a zoomed display right
Left Arrow	Scrolls a zoomed display left
Home	Displays the top-left corner of a zoomed spreadsheet
End	Displays the bottom-right corner of a zoomed spreadsheet

Navigation Keys.

The following keys let you move more easily through notebooks.

SHORTCUT	TASK
Left Arrow	Moves left one cell
Right Arrow	Moves right one cell
Up Arrow	Moves up one cell
Down Arrow	Moves down one cell
Ctrl + Page down	Moves forward one spreadsheet

Ctrl + Page up	Moves backward one spreadsheet
Page up	Moves up one screen
Page down	Moves down one screen
Home	Moves to the upper-left cell (A1) of the active spreadsheet
Ctrl + Home	Moves to the upper- left cell (A1) of the first spreadsheet
End + Home	Moves to the lower-right corner of the filled part of a notebook
End + Arrow key	If the cursor is in a filled cell, the selector moves in the direction of the arrow to the next filled cell before an empty one
Tab	In a notebook, moves right one cell. In a dialog box, moves between controls. In a graphics window, inserts a tab space in text boxes. Press **Ctrl + Tab** to select the next graphic in a chart.
Shift + Tab	In a notebook, moves left one cell. In a dialog box, moves to the previous control. In a graphics window, moves to the beginning of the current word in a text box. Press **Ctrl + Shift + Tab** to select the previous graphic in a chart.
Ctrl + Left Arrow	Moves left one screen
Ctrl + Right Arrow	Moves right one screen

| Ctrl + G, or F5 | Moves to the cell you specify |

Function Keys.

The following list describes the use of each function key when pressed alone, and when pressed together with **Ctrl**, **Shift**, or **Alt**.

SHORTCUT	TASK
F1	Opens Help
Shift + F1	Displays a question mark (?) and a pointer, so you can click a user interface element about which you want information. For example, if you click **Shift + F1** and click a toolbar button, Help for that button displays.
Ctrl + F1	Opens the **Writing tools** dialog box and lets you check the spelling of a document.
F2	Activates Edit mode so you can change a cell entry
Shift + F2	Activates Debug mode so you can execute a macro step by step
Alt + F2	Displays the **Play macro** dialog box
Ctrl + F2	Opens the **Formula composer** dialog box

F3	When you are prompted for cells, or in Edit mode with the cursor positioned after an operator, displays a list of cell names. To expand the list to show cell coordinates, press + (plus sign). Press - (minus sign) to remove coordinates. Press **F3** again to "zoom" the names list to the full screen.
Shift + F3	Displays a list of available macros, by category
Alt + F3	In Value or Edit mode, displays a list of spreadsheet functions, by category
Ctrl + F3	Lets you create a named cell or cell area
F4	In Edit, Value, or Point mode, makes the cell address to the left of the cursor absolute. Press repeatedly to cycle through the eight absolute combinations; for example, $A:$B$4, $A:B$4. You can use F4 when typing or editing a formula.
Alt + F4	Exits Quattro Pro
Ctrl + F4	Closes a window (notebook, dialog box, graphics window, light table window, or dialog window)
F5 or Ctrl + G	Opens the **Go to** dialog box

Shift + F5	Works like the **Quick tab** button next to the spreadsheet tabs ; displays the **Objects** spreadsheet, and then returns to a spreadsheet
Alt + F5	Switches Group mode on and off
F6	If the window is split into two panes, jumps to the other pane
Shift + F6	Displays the previous open window
Ctrl + F6	Displays the next open window
F7	Refreshes output of the previous Notebook query
Shift + F7	In Edit mode, lets you use the **Arrow** keys to select cells containing text
F8	Refreshes output of the previous What-If tables
Shift + F8	Combines selected cells into a group
Ctrl + F8	Separates a group into individual cells
F9	In Ready mode, recalculates the formulas in a notebook. In Edit mode, calculates and displays on the input line the results of formulas. For example, if you type **8*9** on the input line, and press **F9**, the formula is replaced with the result, 72. To recalculate the entire notebook afterwards, press **F9** again in Ready mode.

Shift + F9	Expands the details of a currently collapsed outline group
Alt + F9	Opens the **Data sort** dialog box
Ctrl + F9	Collapses the details of a currently expanded outline group
F10	Works like / or **Alt**; moves the selector to the menu bar.
Shift + F10	Provides a shortcut to the right-click menu
F11	Displays the current chart
Alt + F11	Opens the Visual Basic Editor
F12	Displays the properties for the active cell or cells
Shift + F12	Displays the properties for the active window or notebook
Alt + F12	Displays the properties for the application
Ctrl + F12	Displays the properties of the active spreadsheet

CrossTab Report Keys.

The following shortcut keys can be used in the **CrossTab report** dialog box when creating a CrossTab report.

SHORTCUT	TASK
Tab	Lets you move between different areas of the **CrossTab report** dialog box
Arrow keys	Let you move between the different options in an area of the **CrossTab report** dialog box.
Ctrl+P	Places the selected field in the **Pages** section of the layout.
Ctrl+C	Places the selected field in the **Columns** section of the layout.
Ctrl+R	Places the selected field in the **Rows** section of the layout.
Ctrl+D	Places the selected field in the **Data** section of the layout.
Ctrl+F or Delete	Places the selected field from a section in the layout back in the **Fields** list.
Alt+F	Selects the **Fields** list.

Excel Compatibility Keys.

The following keys are active only when the Microsoft Excel menu is displayed.

SHORTCUT	TASK
F7	Opens the **Writing tools** dialog box and lets you check the spelling in a spreadsheet
Ctrl + K	Opens the **Edit hyperlink** dialog box
Ctrl + H	Opens the **Find/replace** dialog box
Ctrl + R, or Ctrl + D	Opens the **QuickFill** dialog box
Alt + F8	Opens the **Play macro** dialog box
Ctrl + 1	Opens the **Format selection** dialog box

Customer's Page.

This page is for customers who enjoyed Corel Quattro Pro Keyboard Shortcuts.

Dear beautiful customer, we will feel honoured to have you review this book if you enjoyed or found it useful. We also advise you to get the ebook copy of this book so as to access the numerous links in it. Thank you.

Download Our EBooks Today For Free.

In order to appreciate our customers, we have made some of our titles available at 0.00. They are totally free. Feel free to get a copy of the free titles.

Here are books we give to our customers free of charge:

(A) For Keyboard Shortcuts in Windows check:

Windows 7 Keyboard Shortcuts.

(B) For Keyboard Shortcuts in Office 2016 for Windows check:

Word 2016 Keyboard Shortcuts For Windows.

(C) For Keyboard Shortcuts in Office 2016 for Mac check:

OneNote 2016 Keyboard Shortcuts For Macintosh.

Follow this link to download any of the titles listed above for free.

Note: Feel free to download them from our website or your favorite bookstore today. Thank you.

Other Books By This Publisher.

<u>Note:</u> Titles for single programs under Shortcut Matters series are not part of this list.

S/N	Title	Series
Series A: Limits Breaking Quotes.		
1	Discover Your Key Christian Quotes	Limits Breaking Quotes
Series B: Shortcut Matters.		
1	Windows 7 Shortcuts	Shortcut Matters
2	Windows 7 Shortcuts & Tips	Shortcut Matters
3	Windows 8.1 Shortcuts	Shortcut Matters
4	Windows 10 Shortcut Keys	Shortcut Matters
5	Microsoft Office 2007 Keyboard Shortcuts For Windows.	Shortcut Matters
6	Microsoft Office 2010 Shortcuts For Windows.	Shortcut Matters
7	Microsoft Office 2013 Shortcuts For Windows.	Shortcut Matters
8	Microsoft Office 2016 Shortcuts For Windows.	Shortcut Matters
9	Microsoft Office 2016 Keyboard Shortcuts For Macintosh.	Shortcut Matters
10	Top 11 Adobe Programs Keyboard Shortcuts	Shortcut Matters
11	Top 10 Email Service Providers Keyboard Shortcuts	Shortcut Matters
12	Hot Corel Programs Keyboard Shortcuts	Shortcut Matters

13	Top 10 Browsers Keyboard Shortcuts	Shortcut Matters
14	Microsoft Browsers Keyboard Shortcuts.	Shortcut Matters
15	Popular Email Service Providers Keyboard Shortcuts	Shortcut Matters
16	Professional Video Editing with Keyboard Shortcuts.	Shortcut Matters
17	Popular Web Browsers Keyboard Shortcuts.	Shortcut Matters

Series C: Teach Yourself.

1	Teach Yourself Computer Fundamentals	Teach Yourself
2	Teach Yourself Computer Fundamentals Workbook	Teach Yourself

Series D: For Painless Publishing

1	Self-Publish it with CreateSpace.	For Painless Publishing
2	Where is my money? Now solved for Kindle and CreateSpace	For Painless Publishing
3	Describe it on Amazon	For Painless Publishing

www.ingramcontent.com/pod-product-compliance
Lightning Source LLC
Chambersburg PA
CBHW061034050326
40689CB00012B/2810